SERMON OUTLINES FOR

Seekers

By J. Michael Shannon

Standard Sermon Starters

Sam E. Stone, Editor

**STANDARD
PUBLISHING**
Cincinnati, Ohio

The Standard Publishing Company, Cincinnati, Ohio
A division of Standex International Corporation

03 02 01 00 99 98 97 96   5 4 3 2 1

ISBN 0-7847-0525-9

Table of Contents

Introduction

The modern church has re-discovered the seeker. He has always been there, but now we strategize with him in mind. This volume attempts to give assistance to the preacher in creating sermons that reach the seeker. The seeker-sensitive sermon will be composed in the same tension that all seeker-oriented strategies create. How much Bible is the seeker able to assimilate? What are the concerns the seeker wants to hear addressed? How much should we emphasize doctrine?

This volume is produced with the conviction that the seeker is willing to embrace the Bible. Some have been reluctant to allow the seeker to deal much with scriptural material. This is a mistake. He is willing to listen to the Bible, but He doesn't want the material to be presented in a highly technical or impractical manner.

We often hear the admonition, "address the seeker's felt needs." What about his genuine needs, felt or unfelt. This volume is presented with the belief that doctrine is still important, but it must be wrapped in a package that deals with needs.

The sermon outlines contained in this book are of different types. Some messages are topical, some textual, and some expository. Seekers can accept a varied diet.

What makes these messages seeker sensitive is not their structural type, but the way in which they address some issue that seekers express curiosity about. Many of these messages are based on a basic Bible story that many seekers missed in childhood.

These outlines are offered prayerfully, in the hope that they can be combined with the reader's own unique modes of expression that can give seekers genuine guidance.

Affirmative Living

The Life of Joseph

Introduction

Do you have a dream? You need one. Dreams give hope. They display a powerful image of what life can be. Has your dream been shattered? Worse yet, has your dream turned into a nightmare and come true? For all of us dreamers, there is hope.

Joseph was called, derisively, the dreamer. Some of his dreams were prophetic. He saw himself as a leader of men. Joseph dreamed of using his considerable talents to do great things for God and his family. Joseph's dreams enabled him to live affirmatively.

I. Affirmative living means recognizing the presence of God in your life.

A.   Whatever happened to Joseph never caused him to give up on God.

B.   In fact, everything that happened to him only drew him closer to God.

C.   Do you notice the presence of God in your life? Do you believe he has a plan for you? If not, you need to dare to dream again.

II. Affirmative living means making the best of bad situations.

A.   Joseph was hated and sold into slavery. He was unjustly accused and placed in prison. Though forgotten, he never lost hope. We couldn't have blamed him if he had.

B.   But, whatever happened to Joseph, he kept on making the best of it. He was sold into slavery only to become the head servant. Sent to prison, he took over the administration. Brought before the king, he became Pharaoh's right hand man.

C.   Are you faced with troubles that bear down on you? If so, you need to dare to dream again.

III. Affirmative living means maintaining your principles even when inconvenient.

A.   Joseph faced his biggest challenge when accosted by his master's wife.

B.   He could have given all kinds of excuses to give in, but he was willing to do what was right, in spite of the consequences. Have you been mistreated? If so, you need to dare to dream again.

IV. Affirmative living means recognizing God is in control.

A.   Joseph, when he was finally reunited with his brothers, said to them, "What you did to me you meant for bad, God used for good." Joseph believed that ultimately God is in control, and that all things work together for good.

B.   Have you wondered if God has deserted you, or if your life has any purpose at all? If so, you need to dare to dream again.

Conclusion

It is my prayer that God will give you a dream if you do not have one. That he will restore your dream if it has been shattered. That he will give you courage if your dreams have turned to nightmares. Dare to dream again. If you have no dream, you are already dead.

Illustration

If you were to observe a group of people in a downtown area, all walking in different directions, you might think there they had no purpose at all. But if you were to interview each person, you would find that they are going somewhere and there is a purpose in the trip. Likewise, this world seems at times chaotic, but if we had the wisdom, we would see that there is a direction and purpose in life.

Winning Over Worry
Matthew 6: 25-34

Introduction

Worry has become an obsession in our modern world. A look at the self-help section in any bookstore will reveal its prevalence. Hospitals and waiting rooms are filled with people who have physical problems caused by overwhelming anxiety. In addition, there are many people whose lives are disrupted or made unenjoyable because of paralyzing fear.

Christians like to hide their worry by labeling it Christian concern. In spite of protestations to the contrary, Christians do worry. But, do they have to? Not if they learn from Jesus how to win over worry.

Jesus' Sermon on the Mount is intensely practical. He deals with this practical problem of anxiety. If he taught about it, that means he cares about it.

I. There is plenty to worry about (v. 25).

A. There is no shortage of potential items to worry about. Jesus mentions several matters of common concern.
1. Life
2. Health
3. Possessions

B. We could add our own list of concerns.
1. Accidents
2. Aging
3. Weather
4. Criticism

II. There is nothing accomplished by worry (vv. 26-33).

A. It is senseless. The rest of God's creation does not worry, but God provides for them. Will he not do the same for us. This does not say we should not work, only that we should not worry while we work (v. 26, 28).

B. It is fruitless. It will not add an inch to your height or a hour to your life. In fact, it may well take away from your life (v. 27).

C. It is harmful. Worrying makes us look like the heathen, and it destroys our witness. Shouldn't the Christian live differently than those who have no relationship with God (v. 32)?

III. There is a way to defeat worry (v. 33, 34).

A. Trust the heavenly father to provide for us as he has promised (v. 32b).

B. Seek first his kingdom and righteousness and all the things we need will be added to us (v. 33).

C. Live one day at a time. Handle each worry as it comes. Many will never come to pass. Those that do occur can only be handled in the present (v. 34).

Conclusion

Worrying does not prove that we are caring Christians. Worry only proves we do not yet trust God fully. The worry-free life provides freedom for the Christian and a good example for those who aren't. It's hard to imagine Jesus worrying. If we want to be truly Christlike, we must resist the temptation to worry.

Illustrations

An anonymous piece of doggerel says:
Worry is a futile thing
It's something like a rocking chair
It will keep you occupied
But it won't get you anywhere.

A wise man once said, "There ain't no use worrying over what you have control over, because if you have control over it, there's no use worrying about it. There's no use worrying about what you don't have control over, because if you don't have control over it there's no use worrying about it." That covers everything, doesn't it?

Seven Secrets to Spiritual Success
Luke 5:1-11

Introduction

Almost everyone is interested in success. If you have any doubt, look at the business section and self-help section of the local bookstore. Look at the best-selling books. Examine your mail for all the ads for success seminars.

Of all people in the world, Christians should want to succeed. What makes us different are our definition of success and our strategies to get there.

Let's take a lesson from a tired and weary group of fishermen who felt like failures until Jesus taught them a lesson. It was a lesson that sustained them the rest of their lives.

I. Accept the limitations of human efforts and plans.

A.   Peter, Andrew, James and John did all they knew to do and still had come up empty.

B.   While God gave us brains to think with, sometimes we don't have enough cleverness on our own to do the job.

II. Trust the word of Jesus even if it doesn't make sense.

A.   How do you think these fisherman felt, taking advice from a carpenter turned preacher? Didn't they know fishing? It was their business.

B.   Still, there was something in Jesus that caused them to trust him. He did not, of course, ask them to do something immoral, just something that did not seem to make sense.

III. Be willing to take risks.

A.   When Jesus asked them to go out, it was into the deep water.

B.   Every great enterprise takes some risk.

IV. Persevere even through disappointment and fatigue.

A.   The fishermen were tired, but willing to do their part.

B. They were discouraged, but willing to try again.

V. Remember the importance of teamwork.
A. As success came, they had to share the burden.

B. Since Jesus was the ultimate focus, it didn't matter who got the credit.

VI. Remember, God can give us more than we ask or imagine.
A. The catch of fish was even greater than they would have expected.

B. Our God delights in surprising us.

VII. Be humble in your success.
A. Peter did not take credit for the success.

B. In fact, he humbled himself before God and came face to face with His own unworthiness.

Conclusion
Remember after Jesus' resurrection, Peter, in the throes of regret, decided to go back to fishing. Peter no doubt felt he had failed. Jesus came to him again and did a similar miracle. He evidently never forgot the lesson. He went from that place to become a great fisher of men. He became a spiritual success, and so can you. You know the secrets.

Illustrations
Think of how a bird must feel the first time it is pushed from the nest by its mother. The feeling must begin with fear, but as the bird stretches its wings and soars, it becomes exhilaration. Risk is a part of all achievement. A risk-free life is terribly dull.

Runners describe a feeling called the "runners high." It only comes after the runner has pushed past his fatigue and kept on going when every cell of his body is yelling for him to stop. The feeling of exhaustion yields to the feeling of euphoria. It happens only if we are willing to keep on going when we feel like quitting.

People Power
Matthew 7: 1-5, 5:38-42, 5:23-26, 5:43-48, 7:12

Introduction

We can't make it through life without dealing with people. They are everywhere. They are in our homes and at our work. They are at church and where we enjoy our leisure.

Like it or not, we need people. We might wish we could live life totally on our own terms, but that is impossible.

Learning to deal with people will help us at work or at church. It will help us live a happier life. Let's look at some excerpts of Jesus' Sermon on the Mount, to see what principles he can give us for getting along with people.

I. Be careful about judging others (7:1-5).

A. This does not say we cannot or should not discern good from evil.

B. It does say we should not subject others to unreasonable criticism.

C. We are not wise enough to make such criticisms.

D. We are not good enough to make such criticisms.

E. It will keep us busy enough, just monitoring ourselves.

F. If we try to straighten other people out while we have the same problem, then we become as comical as the man with a plank in his eye trying to pick out specks in others' eyes.

II. Do more than expected (5:38-42).

A. Turn the other cheek. This does not mean that we cannot defend our lives. It does mean that we should not take little insults too seriously.

B. Go the extra mile

C. Give another your coat

D. This will drive others crazy until they find out why you are so kind.

III. Don't let disputes fester (5:23-26).

A. It has been said that time heals all wounds, but this is not always true.

B. Sometimes time allows a situation to become worse and worse until it becomes dangerous.

IV. Show kindness to everyone (5:43-48).

A. It is a shame to say sometimes we can't even show kindness to those who are kind to us.

B. Jesus wants us to be kind, even to the undeserving.

C. Showing kindness to an enemy is the ultimate revenge.

V. Treat others as you want to be treated (7:12).

A. This is what has been called the golden rule, for the principle is worth gold to us.

B. Jesus saw this statement as summary of the law and the prophets.

C. Notice that Jesus states this as a positive. He didn't say, "Don't do to others anything you would not want done to you."

Conclusion

People who have people power can be used of God in a mighty way. After all, people are His first concern, and people are His greatest tools.

Illustrations

A lot of us are like the cartoon character, who said, "I love mankind. It's people I can't stand."

Did you hear about the man who had just been won to Christ? A old acquaintance tried to get him involved in a brawl and punched him in the face. The new Christian replied, "You must know that my Lord teaches me that if you strike me on the right cheek, I must turn the other. This I will do. But, you need to know that if you hit the other cheek, he left me no further instructions."

Prayer Pointers

Matthew 6

Introduction

If you wanted someone to instruct you in golf or tennis, wouldn't you choose someone who is good at golf and tennis?

The same goes for prayer. If you want a better prayer life, why not go to someone who excelled in the ministry of prayer? Why not go to Jesus?

One of the topics Jesus taught in the Sermon on the Mount was prayer. What principles for our prayer life can we find there?

I. Prayer should be addressed to God not man (vv. 5, 6).

A. This is not a condemnation of public prayer. Jesus prayed publicly. The Lord's Prayer was a public prayer.

B. It does mean that we must always remember who we are addressing. Prayer time is not a time to try to impress people, but to communicate with God.

C. If we talk to be heard by men, they will hear, but God will not.

II. Prayer is measured by sincerity not multiplication of words (vv. 7, 8).

A. This is not a condemnation of persistence. Later in the sermon, Jesus will recommend persistence.

B. It is condemning empty repetition.

C. It is condemning the notion that the best prayers are the longest prayers.

III. Prayer should follow Jesus' pattern, not our preferences (vv. 9-13).

A. Praise should always come first.

1. Respect for God's names.
2. Commitment to God's kingdom.
3. Submission to God's will.

B. Petition is important but should always come second.

1. Petition for the provision of daily needs.
2. Petition for the pardon of past sins.
3. Petition for the promise of future guidance.

V. Prayer should affect our behavior, not just our mood (v.14).

A. Prayer may make us feel better. While that is welcome, it is not all there is to our prayer life.

B. Prayer will affect the way we relate to other people.

C. If we have received forgiveness from God, it will be difficult not to extend it to others. Something is seriously wrong if we cannot do this.

Conclusion

While prayer is a natural desire of the human heart, it often seems so unnatural. We should not be afraid to accept instruction. Like the disciples of old we cry out, "Lord, teach us to pray." He will do that for you. And you will be able to enjoy a lifetime of close communication and fellowship with God.

Illustration

Bill Moyers, who had previously studied for the ministry, worked in Lyndon Johnson's White House. At one meal, he was asked to say grace. He said it so softly that the boisterous President Johnson said, "Speak up Bill, I can't hear you." Moyers replied, "Mr. President, I wasn't speaking to you."

A little boy got confused saying the Lord's Prayer. Instead of saying "Hallowed be Thy name," he said "Harold be thy name."

Finding Happiness in Strange Places
Matthew 5:1-12

Introduction

The pearl is one of the most precious of gems. It is a miracle of nature. But where does it come from? It is produced by the lowly oyster, an ugly creature, inside and out. The oyster has little in the way of comeliness that would suggest the beauty that resides inside. You can find blessings in strange places.

Jesus proved the truth of that statement, in the spiritual realm, when he preached what we call The Sermon on the Mount. This sermon begins with that familiar word "blessed." Modern translators have often used the words "happy" or "fortunate" instead.

The beatitudes are not a series of commands, but blessings. They are descriptions of the kind of person who will receive the blessings of God. They identify a series of qualities that produce happiness, even though happiness is not readily apparent.

I. Happiness in our relationship to God

A. Jesus says that happiness can be found where there is poverty. The word translated "poor" is the word which denotes absolute poverty. It describes not the condition of having a little, but of having nothing. It is not financial poverty that Jesus has in mind, but spiritual poverty. We must learn to admit our need and to recognize the only one who can fill it.

B. Jesus says that happiness can be found where there is weeping. There is a hidden blessing in mourning. If our heart can be broken, then we know we have a heart. Those who cannot mourn cannot love either. It is better to have a broken heart than no heart at all.

C. Jesus says happiness can be found where there is submission. To the modern mind meekness is a quality to avoid. Meekness is not for the faint-hearted or timid.

D. Jesus says happiness can be found where there is hunger. The hunger referred to here is not the rumble of a missed meal, but the gnawing hunger that results from deprivation. It is not literal hunger, of course, but a hunger and thirst for righteousness.

II. Happiness in our relationship with each other

A. Jesus says happiness can be found where there is forgiveness. Most will agree that mercy is a blessing when you receive it. Jesus says, "Blessed are the merciful . . .."

B. Jesus says happiness can be found where there is sincerity. The non-Christian does not believe that the pure of heart are blessed. The Christian knows a wonderful secret. Purity carries its own reward. It is a lifestyle that brings health and contentment.

C. Happiness can be found where there is conflict. Jesus says, "Blessed are the peacemakers, for they will be called the children of God." You should notice that it does not say, "Blessed are the peace-lovers." If we dare to make peace, then we will be given the greatest compliment a person may know on earth. We will be called "sons of God."

D. Jesus says happiness can be found where there is mistreatment. Everyone wants to be liked; it is our nature. It is not possible to please everyone, especially if you are a Christian. A person who lives a genuine Christian life can be a real nuisance. Persecution can be a character builder. Persecution can make us a more effective witness.

Conclusion

Well, that's the picture of the happy life. How do you like it? You don't have to accept it, you know. But sometime you may find yourself asking, "Is there something more?" Sometime you may find yourself looking for a different kind of happiness. It is at such a time that you may need to start looking for happiness where you least expect it to be.

To receive the blessing of God we must accept a different set of priorities and look in different places than the world would look. You know why. Of course you do. It should be obvious by now. Happiness is found in strange places.

You Can't Have One Without the Other
Matthew 11:17

Introduction

It has been said that you can tell a lot about people if you look at what makes them laugh and what makes them cry. Often laughter and tears dwell together. But what about those who can't do either? Is that a sign of a spiritual problem?

Jesus described the Pharisees as those who could neither dance or cry. This could be a simple description of the Pharisee stubbornness, or it could reveal a spiritual principle we need to recognize.

We think if we had a pain free life we would be closer to God. Adam and Eve knew no pain, yet they felt God was holding out on them. It was when God came to them in their pain that they renewed fellowship.

I. The joy of loving cannot be experienced without the pain of risk.

A. This is true of marriage.

B. This is true of parenthood.

C. This is true of friendship.

II. The joy of accomplishment cannot be experienced without the pain of labor.

A. Athletes teach us this lesson.

B. Musicians teach us this lesson.

C. Laborers teach us this lesson.

D. Spiritual leaders teach us this lesson.

III. The joy of forgiveness cannot be experienced without the pain of contrition.

A. Some try to deny that there is such a thing as sin.

B. We need to take sin seriously, but we also need to take grace seriously.

C. The most wonderful thing that can ever happen to you is to be forgiven.

Conclusion

Jesus experienced this phenomenon. The Bible says, "for the joy that was set before him, Jesus endured the cross." What was that joy? It was the joy of saving you. Remember, sorrow and joy have the same Lord, and he is calling to you today.

Illustrations

"Ye are not above the Master.
   Will you breathe a sweet refrain?
Then His grace will be sufficient
   When your heart is pierced with pain."
                        — Anonymous

Renoir, the famous French painter, in his later years suffered badly from arthritis. On one occasion, his friend Matisse asked, "My friend, why do you keep on painting when you are in so much pain?" Renoir replied, "The pain passes, but the beauty remains."

All Things New
2 Corinthians 5:16-21

Introduction
In everything from computers to dishwashing liquid, we want the new and improved version. Often, however, getting something new is not a luxury, but a necessity. Everyone has experienced the need to replace an old, malfunctioning item with a new one.

Sometimes our broken-down lives also need to be replaced with that which is new and improved.

When Christ came, He replaced the old system with His plan of salvation. He is author of all things new. He wants us to know that our lives can be made new. How are our lives new in Christ?

I. We become a new creation (v. 17).
A. The old things have gone. Do we really believe this? Since we constantly review the past, it is often difficult to accept that God puts our past in the past.

B. The new has come. Do we really believe this? We don't always look new, but where it counts we are.

C. This is only possible because we are in Christ. He is the only one with the power to make us new.

II. We enjoy a new covenant (vv. 18, 19).
A. Once we were separated from God. We were indeed separated, whether we knew it or not.

B. Now we are reconciled to Him. The relationship is mended as if the offense never happened.

C. This is because Christ died for us. This is the beautiful mystery of the cross.

III. We experience a new compulsion (vv. 20, 21).
A. We are reconciled to become reconcilers.

B. We have been made ambassadors.

C. We cannot rest until all who need the message have heard it.

Conclusion

If your life has become dull and boring, if things seem hopeless or meaningless, then go to the God who makes all things new. Let Him change your life.

Illustrations

Augustine of Hippo lived a life of dissipation prior to his conversion. After he had changed his life, he was noticed on the street by a prostitute he had previously frequented. She called to him, "Augustine, it is I." He ignored her while she continued, "Augustine, it is I." Finally he replied, "Yes, but it is no longer I."

When something wonderful happens to us, we can't wait to tell about it. When a couple gets engaged, do they have to be told to tell about it? If he or she won the grand prize, would they have to be urged to tell about it? Why is it Christians seem so shy about telling people about the greatest thing that ever happened to them?

Don't Lose Heart

2 Corinthians 4:1-18

Introduction

Everyone gets discouraged from time to time, and Christians are not exempt.

Paul went through many trials, but he never lost heart. He probably went through greater trials than we will ever experience, so he has a right to instruct us.

Paul told the Corinthians several reasons why they should not lose heart. We can learn from what Paul told them.

Let's look at four reasons why we should not lose heart.

I. The ministry entrusted to us (vv. 1-6)

A. Everyone has a ministry, not just professional church workers. What a great privilege to know that God wants to make us his partners.

B. It is a ministry that flows from God's mercy. Meaning and purpose are great gifts indeed (v. 1).

C. It is a ministry of truth. We have the opportunity to give a trustworthy message to a despairing world (v. 2, 3).

D. It is a ministry that centers on Christ. He is both the subject and the motivation for our work (v. 5).

E. It is a ministry of enlightenment for the world (v. 6).

II. The treasure invested in us (vv. 7-12)

A. The vessel (the body) is weak. Even though we get sick, the message we bring is always alive and vital (v. 7).

B. The vessel is of little value in itself. We are but dust, but the contents of our vessel make us valuable.

C. The vessel does not possess extreme beauty. We may not be beautiful by the world's standards, but the gospel living in us makes us radiant.

D. Because of this, the vessel has great value.

E. Because of this, we can face life's struggles victoriously.

III. The faith working through us (vv. 13-15)

A. Faith is developed by the word of God.

B. Faith is then communicated by us to others.

C. The more we express faith, the more others will find faith.

D. The more people find faith, the more God is pleased.

IV. The character developing in us (vv. 16-18)

A. Inwardly we are constantly being renewed.

B. Compared to eternity, our affliction is short.

C. Our affliction is temporary.

D. We press on as we look forward to eternity.

Conclusion

If anyone had a right to be discouraged, Paul did. He found great joy in how God was using him. If we let God use us, then we need not ever lose heart.

Illustrations

Ponce de Leon went on a fruitless quest for the fountain of youth. What if he had found it? While we might enjoy a longer life, that would not solve our most serious problem. There is a fountain of spiritual youth. It is available to everyone in the word of God.

In the movie, "It's A Wonderful Life," George Bailey's guardian angel asks his superior about George saying, "Is he sick?" The superior answered, "Worse than that, he's discouraged."

Many people have sustained themselves in times of crisis with the little slogan, "This too shall pass." That definitely puts things in perspective. When we look at all our troubles down here, we recognize it is temporary. This too shall pass.

Major Miscalculations

Samson

Introduction

It was a party to end all parties. The main entertainment was a tragic comic display. They called out a blind hulk of a man and forced him to do tricks in front of the drunken crowd. This was not just any old slave, this was their former enemy. His name was Samson.

In the midst of all this, Samson did something he had done little of the rest of his life. He prayed. In that simple prayer he asked God to let him have the last laugh on his enemies. What brought Samson to this terrible, desperate place? It was a series of miscalculations. Samson had more potential than anyone in the Old Testament with the possible exception of Moses, yet he failed miserably. He is the most worthless of the Judges. The excitement of all his adventures does not cover up the tragedy of a wasted life.

I. You can't ignore your heritage without consequences.

A. Samson came from a praying family and was an answer to prayer.

B. He had taken a special vow to be pure and serve God but did not seem to appreciate the significance of this.

C. Today, many also ignore their heritage—some even despising it!

II. You can't unleash your rage without consequences.

A. Samson had an anger that was frequently out of control

B. He seemed to enjoy giving full reign to this anger.

C. In spite of his victories, his anger led him to many sins.

III. You can't forget your promises without consequences.

A. Samson broke his promise to stay pure.

B. He broke his promise to keep ceremonially clean.

C. He broke his promise to keep his symbolic hair long.

E. Promises mean virtually nothing today.

IV. You can't indulge your passions without consequences.

A. Samson's passion caused him to marry poorly.

B. His passion led him to prostitution.

C. His passion led him to his betrayal by Delilah.

D. Sexuality is a powerful urge.

E. Many people have found that failure to control this urge leads to physical, emotional and spiritual problems.

V. He also made one correct calculation in that he knew that God could use him in spite of his failings.

A. Samson believed God could use whatever time he had left, and he was right.

B. Samson believed God could use him no matter how he had failed before, and he was right.

Conclusion

Avoid the mistakes of Samson. He learned the hard way, but you can learn from his example, and that's a lot less painful. But never forget, if you do fail, that God is a God of mercy and grace. Enjoy his grace when you need it, but don't learn your lessons the hard way.

Illustration

All of us have heard the notion of "Safe Sex" proclaimed by the media. Is there any such thing? Some seem to suggest that if you could remove the specter of AIDS, STD's, or unwanted pregnancy, it would be all right for people to have as much sex as they wished. Sex involves more than physical consequences. Sex was given by God and is too powerful and intimate to be shared indiscriminately.

The Great Therefore

Romans 5:1-10

Introduction

Are you a bottom line person? When you are in a business deal, do you want to cut all the talk and get right to the action? Do you have trouble with legal resolutions since they are filled with a lot of *whereas, whereas* and *whereas*? What most of us are really interested in is what comes after the *therefore*. This is what the document is all about.

Paul, in our text, has come to a *therefore*. What is this *therefore* all about? To put it practically, it is telling us what is in it for us. That's a good bottom line question. What are the results of our new relationship to God in Christ? There are many benefits, but Paul lists four to consider.

I. We have enduring peace (v. 1).

A. What kind of peace are we talking about here? It is peace with God.

B. I know it is often peace with others we are striving for. I know that we all try to make peace with ourselves. But, neither of these is possible if we first do not make peace with God.

C. Even if we don't make peace with our neighbor or ourselves, peace with God will solve many of our fundamental needs. How does this peace come about? Jesus himself is the reconciler.

II. We have extraordinary access (v. 2).

A. Isn't is great to have access? The joy of a ticket that lets you get to the best seats in the house is exhilarating.

B. Nothing is more frustrating than to hear or see the words, "access denied."

C. Wonder of wonders, we have access to God and His grace.

III. We have exuberant joy (vv. 2b-4).

A. The joy is notable for its measure. It is a joy so great it gives new meaning to the word.

B   The joy is also notable for its power. It's not just that Christians have joy, but that they have it in the most discouraging situations.

IV. We have eternal hope (v. 5).

A.   Paul says something curious about this hope. He says that it does not disappoint.

B.   Many things in our life disappoint; people, places, books, motion pictures, jobs, churches, etc. But Paul says this hope will not disappoint. He was that sure of heaven.

C.   The reason our hope is secure, is that no matter what happens, or how it looks, God is pouring out His love on us.

Conclusion

So if your concern is, "What's in it for me," I have shown you. If you want joy, access and hope, then accept the gospel today. I think you'll agree that it's the only way to live.

Illustrations

Have you seen the movie, *Shadowlands*? It is a fictionalized account of the relationship between the Christian writer, C. S. Lewis and his late-in-life romance with his wife, Joy Gresham. The movie tries to contrast Lewis' life before marriage with his life after. Everything was tidy. He had all the answers. He lectured on pain and suffering. But, it was a very different thing when he had to experience the pain of losing his wife to cancer. His faith was tested but survived as he learned that the pain is part of the joy.

Handel wrote the majestic joyful passages of *The Messiah* while penniless and half-paralyzed. Even that great work did not get him the job he wanted. Yet there is that majestic phrase, "The Lord God omnipotent reigneth."

A little boy who was confused used to misquote John 3:16. He would say, "God so loved the world that He gave His only begotten son, that whosoever believeth in Him should have ever-laughing life." He was not all wrong, you know.

Decisions, Decisions, Decisions

Hebrews 11: 24-28

Introduction

Everyone I know wants a both a peaceful and fulfilling life. Nevertheless, most people I know feel that in some way life is not cooperating with their desire. Life keeps setting up barriers. The only way to get peace and fulfillment is to make the right decisions about how we are going to conduct our life. We can't control what happens to us, but we can determine the principles we live by.

The fact is, our life is the sum total of our decisions. Some decisions are momentous and some are trivial. Some are easy and some hard. Every day of our life is filled with decisions. How can we make good decisions?

Let's look at the life of Moses as summarized by the author of Hebrews. Here we find that fundamental decisions will determine the quality of our life.

I. Like Moses, we must choose God's plan over our own.

A. The plan of our own making may please us more.

B. The plan of our own making may even seem to make sense.

C. Trying to improve God's plan by substituting our own is ultimate futility.

D. However difficult for us, our plans must yield to his plans.

II. Like Moses, we must choose authenticity over prestige (v. 24).

A. From a worldly perspective, it appears he was giving up everything: all the prestige of the royal family. *in reality we may give up what is bad for us*

B. The things that count greatly in this world are of little concern to God. *Matt 6:33 Seek first the Kingdom of God*

C. Ultimately we all have to settle the question of our identity. Who are we? The answer is that we are God's. *Bottom line the choice of what is real. Our Identity wha are you. God of the world*

31

Choose who you will serve choose who you be

III. Like Moses, we must choose self-denial over pleasure (v. 25).

A. Sin is fun. That may sound shocking, but it is true. Otherwise people would not sin. It is fun but only for a season, and the price we pay later is no fun at all.

B. Sin is usually the easiest choice, but the path of least resistance is often a deadly road. Many lives have been ruined by the inability to say no to that which is dishonorable.

IV. Like Moses, we must choose heavenly rewards over earthly riches (v. 26).

A. In Pharaoh's house, he would have all the riches a man could ever want.

B. Look at the opulence of the pyramids. Moses could have had that kind of wealth. Moses could have been buried there in one of those magnificent tombs.

C. Instead, he is buried in an unmarked grave on a lonely hill in the desert. Still, he made the right choice. God presided at his funeral.

Conclusion

All of us are faced with choices. Written over the fundamental ones are the words "Who chooseth me must give and hazard all he has." Jesus told us that. He said "Whoever finds his life will lose it, and whoever loses his life for my sake will find it." He also said, "Seek first his kingdom and his righteousness and all these things will be given to you as well."

You can Be fulfilled. Remember, the quality of your life is determined by the quality of your decisions. Yes, fulfillment is yours for the taking. The problem is, the choice is up to you.

Illustration

Decisions. Do they ever come hard to you? Are you like the man who had to fill out a job application. One question said, "Do you have trouble making decisions?" The man replied, "Well, yes and no."

Seeing the Invisible
2 Corinthians 4:16-18

Introduction

We have always been curious about seeing the invisible, so we create great microscopes so that we might see microbes and even atoms. We create telescopes so we can see the galaxies and stars so far away.

There are, however, some things we can never see, at least with physical eyes. Some things can only be seen with the eyes of faith.

So much of what is best about Christianity cannot be seen by human eyes. When we do develop our spiritual eyes and are enabled to see what is of the greatest value, then we see that the visible is not worth comparing with the invisible.

I. The visible decay is not worth comparing to the invisible renewal (v. 16).

A. Eventually the human body stops growing.

B. Eventually, little by little, the body ages.

C. As we age, sickness becomes more common.

D. As we age, the pain becomes more intense.

E. This decline never has to happen to our spirit.

II. The visible affliction is not worth comparing to the invisible glory (v. 17).

A. The affliction we must face here is light.

B. The affliction we must face here is temporary.

III. The visible existence is not worth comparing to the invisible existence (v. 18).

A. This life is not all there is. As beautiful as it sometimes can be, God has promised a better place.

B. This life is temporary. Everything we experience here will someday fade, but that which is eternal only grows more beautiful.

C. This life is not the best God has for us.

Conclusion

The most important things in life are things we cannot see. I trust a book, whose original I have never seen, to help me learn about a man I have never met, to save me through an event I have never seen, and take me to a place I have never visited. Nevertheless, I believe.

Illustrations

The country farmer full of country wisdom was talking weather with his neighbors. "Do you think this drought will ever end?" asked one. The wise man said, "I've never seen a drought yet, that didn't end up with a rain."

The county fairs used to gather huge followings. People came to enjoy the rides, shows and food. But, as more people are able to attend the big theme parks like Disney World, Universal Studios, Sea World or Six Flags, the county fair seems less exciting. It's not bad, but it just can't compare.

No Escape
Psalm 139

Introduction

We Christians live under the illusion that everyone wants to find God. This simply is not true. Many people are running away from Him. They need Him—yes; they would be better off with Him—certainly, but they do not want Him. Some people are simply not comfortable with an all-powerful, all-knowing God.

The Psalmist describes his own futile attempt to run away from God. In the end, he finds out there is no escape. Why?

I. There's no escape — God knows too much.

A.   He knows everything we do.

B.   He knows everything we think.

C.   He knows everywhere we go.

D.   This can be frightening, but if the relationship is solid it is also comforting.

II. There's no escape — God is everywhere.

A.   The psalmist tells us if we go as far up as we can or as far down as we can we will not escape God.

B.   The psalmist tells us if we go as far east as we can or as far west as we can we will not escape God.

C.   The psalmist tells us that if we retreat to the dark we will not escape God.

III. There's escape — God's the only one who can help you.

A.   Rather than hiding from God, the psalmist finally says "Search me."

B.   Rather that avoiding God, the psalmist finally says, "Try me."

C.   Rather than resisting God, the psalmist finally says, "Lead me."

Conclusion

When you are in distress, don't be afraid or run away from the footsteps you hear. Those footstep sounds may very well be God. He may be there to rescue you.

Illustrations

If you tried to rescue a wild animal, it might resist you and even defend itself from you with painful attacks. The animal does not realize that resistance may well mean disaster. In fact, the animal needs to discover that in surrender is survival.

Some graffiti artist wrote on a wall, "God is nowhere." A believer came by and with one well-placed slash changed the message to, "God is now here."

What Isaiah Saw

Isaiah 6:1-9

Introduction

Crisis and change often bring people to times of self-examination and reflection and even prayer. It was just such a time for young Isaiah when he went to the temple to pray. King Uzziah's reign had begun with such promise, but unfortunately, pride overtook Uzziah and he presumed to do, in the temple, what was forbidden. He was struck with leprosy and he died, not in the palace, but the leper ward. Any crisis, even a small one, can be an opportunity for a fresh vision of God. If we consider what Isaiah saw, it might help our spiritual eyesight. Like Isaiah, we can find new inspiration and renewed commitment.

I. Isaiah saw his Lord: It was a time of reverence.

A. He needed to see God. He had placed so much confidence in a visible king that he had previously felt little need to reach out to the invisible king.

B. He saw God in all His majesty. God was "high and exalted."

C. He saw God in His power. "The train of his robe filled the temple."

D. He saw God in His holiness. The seraphs, cover themselves in humility. When they sing, they begin with, "Holy, holy, holy." The seraphs' song underscores the fact that we have a holy God. In our desire to stress the love of God, we should never rob Him of His awesomeness.

II. Isaiah saw his sin: It was a time of repentance.

A. This is a natural reaction after coming to terms with the holiness of God. When we capture a vision of God, we must be willing to see ourselves as we really are, even if it grieves us.

B. It is a refreshing thing to see that Isaiah mentioned his own sin before he mentioned the sin of his neighbors. Isaiah saw his own sin and said, "I am a man of unclean lips, and I live among a people of unclean lips."

III. Isaiah saw his cleansing: It was a time of restoration.

A.   God did not deny Isaiah's sinfulness, but he did provide an escape. A seraph took a coal from the altar, where the sacrifice for sin was made, and seared Isaiah's lips, sterilizing them.

B.   There was no reason for Isaiah to continue to feel unworthy. He had been made pure.

IV. Isaiah saw his mission: It was a time of recognition.

A.   When God says, "Go!" we go. There is no debating. We don't say, "There he is, send him."

B.   We don't worry about how the people will respond. Isaiah was warned ahead of time that the people would not respond as they should. It doesn't matter what the people do, we must be faithful.

D.   God sent the people a message not because they wanted it, but because they needed it. The message Isaiah would bring his people was the message he had received. There is forgiveness and purpose with God, if you will just turn your life over to his care and authority.

Conclusion

There is change and chaos in the world, but I say to you, "God is still on the throne." If you doubt it, just look around. He might be closer than you think. Maybe you can say, "I saw the Lord, high and exalted, and that has made all the difference."

Illustration

Many of us are like the man who went to the psychiatrist's office with a fried egg on the top of his head, a strip of bacon draped over each ear, and a sausage link in each nostril. "I need to talk to you, doc," he said, "It's about my brother."

Jesus and the Outcast

John 4:1-26

Introduction

Some of the greatest things in life seem to happen by accident. So it was with Jesus and the woman at the well.

How did this event come together? Neither of them was "supposed" to be there. When you consider the good that was done, you are forced to say, "Maybe it wasn't an accident after all."

Jesus had a remarkable rapport with people who would not appear to make good church members. Notice, Jesus does not condemn, but kindly leads this woman to a faith that would change her life forever.

What can we note here about Jesus and outcasts? That is an important question, for in one way or another we have all been outcasts.

I. Jesus meets us where we are.

A. It is unlikely this woman would have sought Jesus on her own.

B. We can't get to His level, so he comes to us.

C. He meets us at strange times.

D. He meets us at ordinary times.

II. Jesus knows who and what we are.

A. Jesus knew everything about this woman.

B. We can't hide ourselves from Him.

C. That can be troubling or it can be liberating.

III. Jesus loves us as we are.

A. Jesus dealt with this woman gently and sensitively.

B. Sin cannot separate us from His love.

C. How can the one who really knows us love us so much?

D. How did we get the way we are? Only he can tell us.

IV. Jesus cares too much to let us stay as we are.

A. This woman had many problems, and because Jesus loved her he wanted her to have a better life than she had previously known.

B. Jesus loved this woman just as she was; he loved her too much to let her remain in her sad state.

C. He provides for us "living water."

V. Jesus wants to meet our deepest need.

A. Our deepest need is for salvation.

B. Salvation is a gift from him.

C. Salvation is a relationship with him.

VI. Jesus changes us.

A. Once we see who he is and who we are, we can't help but be changed.

B. Once he changes us we can't help but tell others.

Conclusion

Think of how great it would be to find an oasis in the desert. Make sure it's not a mirage or a stagnant pond. Make sure it's living water. Whoever you are, don't be afraid to meet Jesus. He has something to tell you and something to give you.

Illustrations

We all admire the person with the gift to see potential. It is a great skill to look at a young child and say, "He could be a great athlete," "She could be a great doctor," "He could be a great musician," or "She could be a great artist." Jesus had that special insight. He could look at people rejected by the world and say, "She could make a great disciple."

Losing Your Mind

Philippians 2:5-11

Introduction

I want to urge you to lose your mind. Before you say, "Too late; that's already happened," let me clarify. You need to lose your mind so that you might take on the mind of Christ.

Think how many times we see Jesus putting aside His own convenience that he might fulfill the Father's plan. In the garden He said, "Father, everything is possible for you. Take this cup from me. Yet, not what I will, but what you will." Even when He died, we heard Him say, "Father, into your hands I commit my spirit."

Look with me at the beauty of this passage in Philippians. The particular quality of the mind or attitude of Christ is that of humility. While this is not a popular virtue in our day, if we want to be like Jesus, then we need to heed and apply these lessons from His life. What does taking on the mind of Christ mean?

I. Taking on the mind of Christ means surrender (vv. 5, 6).

A. Jesus was willing to surrender the glories of heaven on our behalf. We will never know how difficult it was.

B. We do not mean by surrender giving up in defeat; we mean giving up our agenda. Sometimes that is the only way to win.

II. Taking on the mind of Christ means service (v. 7).

A. Satan's problem is that he would rather rule in Hell than serve in Heaven.

B. Jesus was willing to come to earth and serve humanity.

C. Jesus did not consider service to be a sign of weakness.

D. Service must be voluntary or it is not service.

III. Taking on the mind of Christ means sacrifice (v. 8).

A. No great accomplishment was ever made without sacrifice.
   1. That is true in science.
   2. That is true in politics.
   3. That is true in religious reform.

B. Not only did Jesus die on a cross, He told us we will have to bear one.
    1. Our cross does not consist of the common troubles and difficulties of life.
    2. Our cross consists of those things we voluntarily endure for the cause of Christ.

IV. Taking on the mind of Christ means certainty.

A. It means betting your life on God.

B. The day of His crucifixion, everyone was afraid except Jesus.

C. Trust is tested at such a time as this.

D. We believe that God can bring great beauty and victory out of the cross.

E. Jesus was honored for his humility, and it is pleasing to God when we are humble.

Conclusion

If Jesus was not afraid to be humble, then it is the height of absurdity for us to be arrogant. The principle remains: "Whoever exalts himself will be humbled and whoever humbles himself will be exalted" (Matthew 23:12).

Illustrations

John Bowring was visiting in the Orient. He passed by a village destroyed by earthquake. Out of the rubble of an old church he saw the cross. It inspired him to write the great hymn, "In the cross of Christ I glory, towering o'er the wrecks of time."

Said a coach to a baseball player who failed to put down the sacrifice bunt, "Didn't you see the sign, didn't you see me say sacrifice?" "Yes, I saw it," said the player, "I just didn't think you meant it." When God tells us to sacrifice, he means it.

I Doubt It

Matthew 11:1-11

Introduction

"I doubt it." These three little words have become a byword for our age. We have become the age of the question mark. It's not that people find believing in the possibility of the supernatural difficult. People today choose to believe in all kinds of supernatural things except Jesus and the Bible.

Actually a little doubt wouldn't hurt if applied to the superstitious and the cultic. It may be that doubt is a doorway to true faith.

Submitted to you today is the story of John the Baptist. John emerges as the voice crying in the wilderness. He was not afraid to take on the powers that be. Herod arrests John, and he is now alone and in prison. That is enough to discourage any man. He is facing death. Let's learn along with John something about what happens when a believer says, "I doubt it."

I. It's all right to come with honest questions.

A. Some people say that we should never question our faith, but they are wrong; that is superstition. Jesus never gives any word of rebuke to John.

B. John is the man who said, "Behold the Lamb that takes away the sin of the world." John is the man who said, "I am not worthy to untie his sandals." John is the man who said, "He must become more and more and I must become less and less." Now he says, "Are you the one?"

C. Sometimes doubt is intellectual. John may have needed simple reassurance. Sometimes doubt is emotional. John may have been thinking, "I was the forerunner. I have deferred to you, and this is how I get treated."

D. Notice that Jesus is not the least bit afraid of honest doubters. Do we think our faith is so fragile that it can't stand up to a few questions?

E. He described John as the greatest man ever born of woman. That's quite a compliment from Jesus. Notice John does not say, "Are you the one, or do we give up?" He says, "Are you the one, or shall we expect someone else?" That is faith.

II. It's important to ask the right kind of questions.

A. John is not asking about trivial things. He has gone to the heart of the matter.

B. If we are going to take time out to question our faith, let us make sure that the issues before us are monumental, not trivial.

C. The question of the identity of Jesus is indeed crucial to the Christian faith.

III. It's crucial to take your questions to right person.

A. If you have a question, go to an expert.

B. Whatever doubts John had about Jesus, he still believed Jesus would give him the right and honest answer.

C. Jesus' teaching and insights have been repeatedly proven to be dependable.

D. Why do some believe everything Jesus taught, except what he taught about himself?

IV. There are answers to your questions.

A. You might not get your answers in a mathematical formula or under a microscope, but there are answers for the person who comes in the right spirit.

B. Jesus does not debate the questioners. He gives them a simple response, "Tell John what you have seen and heard." Only Jesus would dare make such a reply.

C. Where else can we go for our answers? Is there anyone else you are willing to trust your life to?

Conclusion

Is our God so puny that he trembles at our questions? Is faith so feeble that it falters before the question mark? Will our Christianity crumble into pieces because we have a few questions? I doubt it.

The Comfort Connection

2 Corinthians 1:3-7

Introduction

People often ask why God allows suffering. While this is an intriguing question, we will never be able to answer it adequately. Countless people have also experienced the comfort of God. We can't explain that either, but we can experience it. If we are going to blame God for the suffering, then we ought to thank him for the comfort we have received. Let's examine Paul's thinking together and see what Paul teaches us about comfort.

I. What God allows — tribulations (vv. 3, 4a).

A. The Bible never promises a life without problems. The way some people act and talk you might think such a promise has been made, but it has not.

B. The Bible specifically states that we will face trouble. God did not leave us to discover this truth by ourselves. He warned us in the word that we would suffer.

II. What God promises — comfort (vv. 3, 4b).

A. While he does not promise a trouble-free life, God does promise that He will comfort us in all our troubles.

B. He is described as the Father of all compassion. Any act of kindness is ultimately reflective of God's love.

C. He is the God of all comfort. Any feeling of comfort is ultimately prompted by God.

III. What God expects — caring (vv. 5-7).

A. If we have received comfort from God, then we should share it with others. After all, we should remember how God used other people to bless us.

B. In turn, others will share comfort with us when we need it. As we sow, so shall we reap. We set up a cycle of goodwill and blessing.

C. How can it be that anyone who received comfort should be stingy in giving it to others? When we know how precious the gift is, we should be prompted to reproduce it over and over. Will you dare to become a part of the Comfort Connection? Someone's life may depend on it.

Conclusion

God has made a great provision for our lives. We need to know that we can receive help whenever we need it from our Christian brothers and sisters and from God as well.

Illustration

Many times, when we face trouble, we are prone to ask, "Why me?" That is understandable, but upon further reflection we should be able to say, "Why not me?"

She was a young woman who desperately wanted to bear children. After much prayer it seemed certain she would not. After much heart-wrenching consideration, she decided to turn around her bitterness and begin training to become an obstetrics nurse. She finds great satisfaction in helping others safely through childbirth. God will either change our circumstance or change us. Either is a great blessing.

Have you noticed the phenomenon of the support group? What is the theory behind it? It is hoped that those who have been through a problem (e.g. childlessness, cancer, phobias, addiction, etc.) can be of help to others going through the same problem. The Bible describes this very thing as a ministry and outreach of the church. No one understands what you are going through like someone who has been there.

Make Way for the Word
James 1:19-25

Introduction

Seminaries and Bible Colleges try very hard to turn tongue-tied young people into dynamic communicators. They teach all the best methods, provide practice and give critiques.

There is, however, a part of the process the preacher has no control over and that is the attitude of the hearer. In the parable of the sower, it is the soil and not the seed that determined the level of productivity. James is well aware of these problems.

In light of this James gives practical advice in how to respond the word of God.

I. Preparation for the Word (1:19-21a)

A. The first step in the preparation for the Word is to "be quick to listen." He who is listening is learning.

B. The second step in preparation is to be "slow to speak." Constant speaking means we aren't in a mode to receive information.

C. The third step in preparation to be "slow to anger." The ability to defeat anger allows us to listen to unpleasant truths. When we are angry, our thinking is out of balance; our reasoning is undependable.

D. The last step of preparation is to "get rid of all moral filth and the evil that is so prevalent." If we are nurturing secret sinful thoughts, it is difficult to accept the truth of God.

II. Reception of the Word (1:21b)

A. First, we must take the word seriously. God has given man a great but risky responsibility. He lets us decide if we will accept His Word or not.

B. James then says we must "humbly accept" the authority of the word. The attitude of humility is really a prerequisite. We need to let God's Word rule over us, not us rule over it.

C. We must understand the power of the Word. The power of the
    living God stands behind it. The Word has the power to convict
    and save.

III. Application of the Word (1:22-25)

A. Do not merely listen to the Word; do what is says. A lot of peo-
    ple who claim to live under the authority of the Word have never
    put what they know into practice.

B. Use the Word like a mirror.
    1. You go to the mirror to get an accurate appraisal.
    2. You go to the mirror to see what needs to change.
    3. You go to the mirror to change it.

C. Receive the word like a law. James describes the Word of God as,
    "The perfect law that gives freedom."
    1. The first thing to note is that the law of God is perfect. No
        human law can make that claim.
    2) Secondly, note that it is a law that gives freedom. Law and
        freedom seem contradictory to us. Laws tell us what we can-
        not do, and freedom speaks of what we can do. But, there is
        no freedom without a law that protects or provides it.

Conclusion

God cared enough for us that he sent us his instructions. We need to
take his Word seriously. It is not just an academic study. It is the key
to both eternal life and abundant life.

Illustrations

A wise man once said that we have two ears and one mouth, so that
ought to be the ratio of listening to speaking.

Traffic laws enable us to be free to drive safely. What if everyone
decided to interpret the red light for himself. What if a driver said, "To
me, the red means *go*"? The result would be utter chaos.

What if a football team arbitrarily decided that it takes only five yards
to get a first down or that a touchdown would be one hundred
points? The freedom to play the game depends on adherence to the
laws.

Keep Hope Alive

1 Peter 1:3-9

Introduction

Sometimes in spite of all the positive thinking we can generate, life is really terrible. Simple optimism will not do. Genuine hope must go beyond positive thinking. Genuine hope is not, "Wishing for something you know isn't going to happen." It is not an idle wish at all.

I. The origin of genuine hope (v. 3a)

A. All real hope is derived from God and his promises.

B. It is a gift of his mercy.

C. Genuine hope is a result of our salvation. We were born into a living hope.

II. The foundation of genuine hope (v. 3b)

A. The foundation is the work and ministry of Jesus Christ.

B. The resurrection of Jesus is particularly crucial in the formation of genuine hope. It makes all the difference.

III. The durability of genuine hope (v. 4)

A. It is incorruptible. This speaks of its essence.

B. It is undefileable. This speaks of its purity.

C. It is unfading. This speaks of its beauty.

IV. The power of genuine hope (vv. 6, 7)

A. It helps us to face our trials with courage.

B. It helps us to face our trials with joy.

V. The wonder of genuine hope (vv. 8, 9)

A. We love a person we have never seen.

B. We long to go to a place we have never visited.

C. Genuine hope concerns our greatest need — salvation.

Conclusion

Hope is a powerful concept. Without hope in the future, we have no power in the present. Hope may keep us alive. Without hope there is no reason to live. It has been said, "Life without Christ is a hopeless end, but life with Christ is an endless hope."

Illustrations

She was a hospice nurse. She had ministered to many as they faced death, trying to ease the transition. A minister asked her, "Do Christians die differently from others?" "Most definitely, yes," she replied, "Christians really do die better." Why do Christians die better? They know it isn't over.

A student athlete was contemplating the height of the bar on the high jump. "I don't think I can make it," he said. "Think positive!" said a friend. "All right," the athlete said boldly, "I'm positive I can't make it."

Hooray for Trouble
James 1:2-5

Introduction

Hooray for trouble! That sounds ridiculous doesn't it? Yet that is in essence what James says when he tells us to count it all joy when we face trials of various kinds. What kind of crazy man would give us this kind of advice? Maybe he's not crazy at all — just inspired.

None of us doubts for a moment that some day we will have to face difficult times. The issue is not "if" we face suffering, but "when." In the passage of scripture before us, James tells us how to respond in the face of suffering.

I. Respond positively (v. 2).

A. Some choose to respond to trouble with rage.
  1. This might make us feel better temporarily, but in the long run it will not satisfy.
  2. When we are in a state of rage, we do more harm than good.

B. Some choose to respond to trouble with resignation.
  1. Just giving in will certainly not solve the problem.
  2. Just giving in will not make us feel any better.

C. James tells us to respond to trouble with rejoicing.
  1. We don't have to rejoice for the trouble in and of itself.
  2. We can rejoice over the good things the trouble can make happen in our lives and in our world.

II. Respond productively (vv. 3, 4).

A. Let trouble help you develop patience.

B. Let trouble help you develop perseverance.

C. Let trouble help you develop maturity.

III. Respond prayerfully (v. 5).

A. Some might pray for deliverance, and there is nothing wrong with that.

B. Some might pray for a change of the circumstances, and there is nothing wrong with that.

C. Sometimes, however, what we really need is wisdom.
    1. We must ask God for this wisdom.
    2. He will give generously.
    3. He will give without finding fault.

Conclusion

If it takes a broken heart to draw us closer to God, then our prayer should be, "Break my heart." Anything that draws us closer to God has great value. So you see, we really can say, "Hooray for trouble."

Illustrations

Do you have wind chimes at your house? The next time you face a storm, listen carefully. Along with the howling wind, you might hear a beautiful sound from the chimes. They are making music in the midst of a storm. That is a parable of our lives. In the face of the greatest storms of our lives, we can make beautiful music.

If you want to see what's in a sponge — just squeeze it. The contents will reveal themselves under pressure. The same thing will happen to you. When the pressure gets tough, you will see what's inside your heart and soul.

Hungry for the Word
1 Peter 1:22—2:3

Introduction

Is it possible that *Time* magazine was right, when they described the Bible as a book "more revered than read"?

The Bible needs to be treasured, but more than that it needs to be internalized. Peter has much to say on the importance of the Word for spiritual health.

I. The Significance of the Word (v. 25).

A. It is not of human origin; it is the Word of God.

B. It is eternal.

II. The Desire for the Word (v. 2).

A. Like a child who cries for milk, we must be single-minded in our desire for the truth of Scripture.

B. People can, if they so choose, satisfy their craving inappropriately. They can abuse themselves by taking in junk food. They temporarily satisfy their hunger with poor or even dangerous substitutes.

III. The Inhibitors of the Word (v. 1).

A. There are diseases that interfere with the process of absorbing food. There are also diseases that interfere with the absorption of the Word.

B. Peter says, "Rid yourselves of all malice and all deceit, hypocrisy, jealousy, and slander of every kind." The wrong attitudes can devastate the work God wants to accomplish. Our mind is not ready to receive instruction because we have so many distractions.

C. More than just distractions, these attitudes run totally contrary to the spirit that results from compliance to the Word.
    1. If you hate, you close yourself off to your neighbor and to God.
    2. If you are dishonest, then the teaching of Scripture will hold little authority over you.

3. If you are a hypocrite, then you can recite the words without any genuine commitment.
4. If you are filled with jealousy and slander, you distance yourself from God's people and his happiness.

IV. The Substance of the Word (v. 2, 3).

A. The Word of God is described as pure and pleasant. To say that it is pure is to say that no evil teaching can be found in it. We can depend on scripture to nourish us and not poison us.

B. The Word is also described as pleasant. Granted, some parts seem "sweeter" than others. Like children, we are not always able to appreciate its taste.

V. The Effect of the Word (v. 2).

A. Peter says that we will grow up in our salvation if we internalize the word.

B. Among other things it means growth in knowledge.
1. It is certain that the Bible will teach us about our world. If historical matters alone are considered, the Bible is an invaluable book.
2. No other book so effectively teaches us about man. Customs may have changed, but passions have not. If we are ready to receive it, the Bible will teach us about ourselves.
3) But above all, the Bible teaches us about God and salvation. No other book can do that.

C. The Bible will also help us grow in wisdom. No man, Christian or not, can consider himself a wise and educated man if he does not know something about Scripture.

D. Finally, the Bible will help us grow in faith. How can anyone grow in faith without regular consumption of the Word?

Illustration

John Locke once said, "The Bible is one of the greatest blessings bestowed by God on the children of man. It has God for its author, salvation for its end, and truth without mixture for its matter. It is all pure; all sincere; nothing too much; nothing wanting."

Who Is This Jesus?

Matthew 16:13-20

Introduction

It is probably the most important question in the world. That question is, "Who is Jesus?"

The question was so important Jesus even asked the question to His disciples. In a sense, He asks it of all of us.

I. The Great Question (v. 13).

A. Notice the significance of the place where He asked the question.
  1. Pagan temples surrounded the area.
  2. There was a Roman garrison there.

B. Notice the significance of the occasion He asked the question.
  1. Others had left Jesus.
  2. The cross was ahead.
  3. He wanted to know the depth of the disciples' faith.

C. Notice the significance of the words He spoke.
  1. He began with a general question.
  2. He moved to a personal question.

II. The Great Answer (vv. 14-16).

A. There were many wrong answers.
  1. They said, "Some say you are a prophet."
  2. They said, "Some say you are John the Baptist."
  3. Today some say He is a rabbi.
  4. Today some say He is a guru.
  5. Today some say He is a great revolutionary.
  6. Today some say He is a religious reformer.

B. What are the right answers?
  1. He is the Christ.
  2. He is the Son of God.

III. The Great Promise (v.18).

A. I will build my church.

B. It will never be defeated.

C. I give you the keys to the kingdom.

Conclusion

Try as it may, this world can't shake Jesus. Even those who do not believe in Him, are compelled by Him. If you believe He was a great teacher, then hear His teachings concerning Himself. Take great care, for this is the most important decision you will ever make. The Christian faith stands or falls on the person of Jesus Christ. So I ask each of you, who do *you* think He is?

Illustrations

Napoleon said, "I know men and Jesus is no mere man."

C. S. Lewis once said that Jesus couldn't be a great teacher if He claimed to be the Son of God and was not. That would make Him a lunatic, like any man who says he's a boiled egg. Beyond that he would be a devil.

Don't Miss the Party
Luke 15:11-32

Introduction

Almost everyone likes a party. Almost no one associates Christianity with a party, but Jesus did. He talked about rejoicing in Heaven when a sinner repents; about the kingdom of Heaven being like a king who holds a great feast; and about Heaven being like a wedding supper.

The Bible is full of the imagery of parties, but it is possible to miss the party. Jesus tells us how. It comes at the end of the parable of the prodigal son. A younger bother takes his inheritance and wastes it. He trades his self respect for a pig pen. There, he learns a great lesson. Life can begin in a disaster that reveals our need for God.

A wandering, shivering boy returns penniless, willing to become a mere servant in his father's house. When the father sees him in the distance, he runs to greet him. Before the boy can deliver his well-rehearsed speech, he is wrapped up in his father's grace. The father, so happy to see his son, kills the prized calf and hosts a party, with music and dancing.

The older son, who stayed home, comes out of the field and refuses to go in. He is now a prodigal of sorts himself. One son ran away from home; another refused to go home. Outside the house is outside the house, regardless of how one gets there. This older brother missed the party. Why?

I. He did not understand his father's kindness.

A. Can't we understand the elder brother's anger? It does seem like a raw deal. While the younger son was sowing wild oats, the elder brother was sowing the crops. How can the father be so kind to the undeserving?

B. No doubt he said to himself, "So this is how you get recognition in this house. Run away, waste money, drink, and party." Rather than celebrate his father's kindness as a virtue, he condemned it as a vice.

II. He did not understand his brother's transformation.

A. The younger brother really is a changed man. He has exhibited real repentance. It took a lot to admit he was wrong. He did not come home demanding, but begging. He left home saying, "Give me"; he came home saying, "Forgive me."

B. The elder brother never really considered that his brother had changed.

C. The younger son was treated to a real party, unlike the pale imitations he experienced in the far country. But the elder brother would, and I would too, force the boy to go to his room without supper. Make him sit in his room and consider what he has done. But, in the act of returning, he was repenting.

III. He did not understand his own position.

A. First, nothing he has will be taken away. Whatever privileges he has are still his. And righteousness has its own rewards. He never had to go hungry. He never had to face the degradation of the far country.

B. Secondly, though his behavior is "good" there is a problem in his heart that can only be described as "sin." He too needs to depend on his father's mercy. The party is a celebration of grace, a gift he, too, can receive.

Conclusion

The older brother is so angry he misses all the fun. He is not, however, shut out of the banquet hall. He has locked himself out. The father will let him in . He probably does not even realize that a place has been set for him at the table. There is a plate filled for him. They probably saved him a piece of cake, if he only had the sense to go in.

Three Cheers for God
Ephesians 1:3-14

Introduction

Have you ever noticed the changes that take place when you get really excited? We smile more, we move faster, and our speech is greatly affected. We feel like shouting.

Paul gives us a long song of praise in this passage. In fact, this whole text is one long sentence in the original language of the New Testament.

His song should be our song. In a sense he is saying, "Three cheers for God."

I. The first cheer: Thank you God, for choosing me.

A.   God chooses those who choose His son.

B.   It is a great privilege to be chosen.

C.   It is a great responsibility to be chosen.

D.   Most of all, it is a great joy to be chosen.

II. The second cheer: Thank you God, for saving me.

A.   We have been adopted into the family of God.

B.   We have been redeemed from the bondage of sin.

C.   We have been forgiven from the penalty of sin.

III. The third cheer: Thank you God, for sharing with me.

A.   God does not just save us and then leave us alone.

B.   He has shared with us the gift of the Holy Spirit so that we might grow in the faith.
    1.   The Holy Spirit is the Father's mark of ownership.
    2.   The Holy Spirit is the Father's promise of fellowship.

Conclusion

We should be like spiritual pop bottles. What's in us should build up until we explode with joy over what the Father has done for us. All we can say is "Hip, Hip, Hooray."

Illustrations

Gerald Ford was born Leslie King. He was adopted and grew up in the Ford family. As a young man, Ford met his birth father who wanted him to change his name back. Ford said no. His adopted family was his real family.

A lady was once asked about how she felt. She said, "I feel so good I can hardly keep myself from smiling." She didn't have to restrain it. Joy is a proper response to all God has given us.

When people play golf, they often give each other a "mulligan." This is granted when a person's shot is so bad, only a new start will do. The mulligan is a nice courtesy, but golf is only a game. In the Christian life, the new start is absolutely essential.

It Costs to Serve Jesus

Matthew 8:18-22

Introduction

Jesus never wanted to accept disciples under false pretenses, so he always let them know what was the price of discipleship. Jesus was attractive and winsome. He did not want crowds to follow him without an appreciation of what they would have to give up. Jesus wanted to separate the casual from the consecrated disciples.

We sing, "It pays to serve Jesus." That is true enough, but it also costs to serve Jesus. What are the prices too high for the "summer soldier and sunshine patriot"? What are the barriers to discipleship?

I. There is the barrier of personal comfort.

A.   The first would-be disciple in our passage would not follow because he would have to give up some creature comforts. What about you?

B.   The gospel is simple, but it is not easy. It calls people to move to a mission field or give of their treasure.

C.   There are many people willing to be in the army as long as they only march in parades. Very few are willing to march into battle.

D.   The gospel may very well make you comfortable in some areas. More than making you a happy person though, the gospel wants to make you a fulfilled person.

II. There is the barrier of misplaced priorities.

A.   The second would-be disciple felt the call of family ties over the call to discipleship. (Note: Jesus was not denying this man a chance to go to his father's funeral. He used an expression which meant "Wait until my father dies.")

B.   Some, like this man, make family the focus of their lives.

C.   Some make work the focus of their lives.

D.   Some make leisure the focus of their lives.

E.   Some make self the focus of their lives.

F.   Where is God in all of this?

G. Not all these things are bad in themselves, but become bad when they keep us from being Jesus' disciple.

III. There is the barrier of procrastination.

A. We often try to put off any decision whatsoever.

B. We often put off decisions because they are limiting.

C. We often put off decisions because they are risky.

D. Not to decide is to decide, and it is a way to say, "No."

E. Too many people don't so much decide against Jesus as fail to decide for him.

Conclusion

Yes, there are benefits to living the Christian life. Those benefits are significant. Those benefits do not come except to those who will pay the price. Remember, ministry that costs nothing accomplishes nothing.

Illustrations

G. K. Chesterton said, "Christianity has not been tried and found wanting. It has been found difficult and not tried."

A moping soldier, walking aimlessly, was confronted by his sergeant, "What are you doing?" asked the sergeant. "Just procrastinating sergeant," said the soldier. "O.K. then," said the sergeant, "just so I know you are busy."

It was Dietrich Bonhoffer who reminded his readers that when Jesus calls us, he calls us to come and die. Bonhoffer's most famous work was entitled *The Cost of Discipleship.*

Triumphing Over Temptation

1 Corinthians 10:1-13

Introduction

A man had a sign on his door which said, "Lead me not into temptation, I can find it for myself." We can all make that statement. Temptation will make itself known on a daily basis.

Since it is very easy to find temptation, we should consider Paul's advice in 1 Corinthians, chapter 10, so that we can learn how to gain victory.

Paul's advice consists of warnings drawn from the history of the children of Israel. These events are so ancient they may seem foreign to us, but they do speak to universal tendencies and needs. Even though the Israelites lived in close fellowship with God, they found themselves tempted.

Let's go on a scouting report, so that we may see what temptation is and how it may be defeated.

I. Facing temptation (vv. 1-10).

A. There is the temptation to dethrone God (v. 7).

B. There is the temptation to give in to lust (v. 8).

C. There is the temptation to test God (v. 9).

D. There is the temptation to grumble (v. 10).

E. These are not the only temptations, but they are all still among us today.

II. Fighting temptation (vv. 11-13).

A. We must be constantly vigilant — temptation will come (vv. 11, 12). It shouldn't catch us by surprise, but it often does.

B. We must be constantly hopeful — temptation can be defeated (v. 14). We need not despair. God gives us the tools necessary to say, "No."

   1. God will not allow us to suffer any temptation we cannot bear. At times, it may seem that we cannot bear it, but we must believe that we can, because we really can.

2. God will always provide a way of escape. Like Joseph we need to keep our eyes on the exit. There will be an escape provided, if we will watch for it and use it.

Conclusion

We will never triumph over temptation pretending it doesn't exist. We cannot afford the luxury of thinking it can't happen to us. Thanks be to God who can give us the victory over temptation.

Illustrations

Temptations will come and they are not in themselves sins. If they were, then Jesus would have been a sinner for He was tempted as we are. Nevertheless, the time of temptation is a time for vigilance. Martin Luther said, "You can't keep the birds from flying overhead, but you can keep them from building a nest in your hair."

Ancient mythology tells of the sirens' call. They were beautiful sea maidens who enticed a ship to sail close by singing a beautiful song. The ship would then wreck on the rocks. Many a soul has been lured to ruin by what at first seemed beautiful.

Temptation is like the Turkish Delight candy in C. S. Lewis' *The Lion, the Witch and the Wardrobe.* One boy found it irresistible. The more he ate, the more he wanted, but the less he liked it.